In this article, a little longer than normal, I am going to develop points 9, 9.1, 9.2 and 9.3 of the book that I wrote dismantling the elite manifesto for true freedom where I expose an alternative system to

capitalism that has little to do with the communisms as we have known them. The system is a communism 2.0 without leaders of the revolution and using technology to distribute wealth (everything that is produced), eliminating money and legislating among everyone through an app of constant referendums, eliminating obsolescence programmed for the long run. working fewer hours and guiding society through studies and research without economic interests involved.
Real equality for all.
Why eliminate money?
The capitalist system is based on money, on the

creation of money and on the struggle of companies and people to get hold of it and in which very few people manage to achieve wealth and abundance (which no one dislikes) but It generates enormous inequality and the suffering of almost 99% of humanity who see how the richest 1% live and who suffer from not having access in many cases to the most basic things such as housing, healthcare, education or transportation. drinking water.

Also, since capitalism is based on money and the free market, there are very clever people and historically in their families with a lot of

power who acquire large amounts of money and all this money and this power they use for their personal interests, not for those of the common good buying media, politicians and ultimately making the world a place in which "4" people decide how 8,000 million are going to live and it is clear that they do not think about us or our good, they think that they have to do so that their business is not screwed up, manipulating people and dividing and polarizing society so that it does not unite in a revolution against them.
Even in real communism there is no room for money since it would be the capitalism of the

leaders of the revolution.
In communism there is
room for apples, pears,
lettuce, tomatoes, clothes,
even cell phones, but not
money.
That is why in my system I
propose to create a
computer system that
distributes everything that
is produced equally among
everyone, thus replacing
money and people with a
large amount of money
and power.
This computer system
would take into account
the global production of
each product and each
individual's consumption
of that product.
It would be an artificial
intelligence that, through
an app and a card, would
release products to you

that you want to consume
and the limit would be
how many similar
products other people
besides you consume.
All production would have
to be put into the system
and the system should also
organize the movements of
merchandise and imports
and exports taking into
account the amount of
each thing that is usually
consumed in each
territory, managing
everything in an efficient
way, with local
consumption being the
that rewards
If, for example, the system
says that you can drink 50
beers a month, it is
because it takes into
account the beer
production of that year

and the amount of beers
consumed by the rest of
the population, and if you
want to drink more beers
you cannot because you
simply cannot. You would
be taking someone else's
beers and in this system
we have talked about
being all equal.
It would be an artificial
intelligence system that is
complicated to create but
possible in 2023.
This system could even
determine which crops
should be planted taking
into account the demand
for common products or
new trends, but in this
system no one would
benefit from the sale of
products, becoming a
millionaire, but rather
things would be as they

are, an apple is an apple.
apple, not €1, 10% taxes
and 20% profit for the
person who sells it to you.
An apple is what I need
and the system gives it to
me, if it corresponds to
me, we are all obliged to
work but we have our
basic needs covered.
In the capitalist system if
you don't have money you
can't even eat.
Why without leaders of
the revolution?
Because through an app of
constant referendums we
legislate among everyone.
You can create a
legislative proposal at the
neighborhood, city,
autonomous community,
state, European or global
level and this proposal
passes a filter if it is

shared or given many likes
in relation to the people
who have to vote for it.
For example: if I create a
proposal for my
neighborhood: the
txantrea because there is a
traffic sign that is poorly
placed on one side of the
street where no driver sees
it and many vehicles turn
in the opposite direction,
then I can create a
proposal to change the site
sign, if it is proposed, it is
given many likes or shared
many times in relation to
the people who have to
vote for it, (the inhabitants
of the txantrea) through
an algorithm that
determines that there is
interest in that proposal It
would go to the voting
menu and the people of

the txantrea would vote
for it with a yes or no.
If it comes out, the
proposal would be
transferred from the app
to the city council, with the
officials being the ones
who execute that proposal,
but it would not be the
mayor who decided to
change the signal but
rather the inhabitants of
the txantrea, who are
really responsible for
ensuring that the signal is
there. Well set.
In this system, if we do not
want the mayor or the
president or the leader of
the revolution to do their
job (we all know that
corruption exists), we
must all do the mayor's
job, so in this system we
should all be obligated. for

example, to vote on all the legislative proposals that concern us in the territory in which it is, taking us perhaps an hour a day.

It is clear that someone who wants something has a hard time, and on the other hand, if we eliminate planned obsolescence and engineers design products to last, we would work many fewer hours in the long run since fewer products would have to be produced.

The media has no place in this system due to its high capacity to influence the decisions that people make to vote in the referendum app, but a social network without censorship and without bots would have a place (you could only

create an account with
your DNI) and this social
network could serve to
inform you. It could also
be a social network in
which together we classify
each publication as hoax
or real.
For example, if I want to
publish news about
something that happened
in my neighborhood, the
social network can take
the location from where
the photo was taken to
complete this news and
can know that I really was
there when that happened.
In addition, the rest of the
users can give veracity to
the news or facke news,
with each publication that
you put, for example, 80%
real, taking into account
what each user who has

seen the news has determined about it and taking into account the time of publication. the facts and location of each user who has rated the news their location.
Another important aspect to take into account is how work is organized.
An organization would have to be created to manage jobs in each territory and if, for example, a person wants to change jobs, they would have to enter a lottery to be awarded a new position. Job rotations could be allowed, for example every 3 years, and the most sacrificial and important jobs such as livestock or agriculture should be done by

practically everyone but for a few hours. For example, each person in each autonomous community has to go to work in the fields one week a year.

An effort should be made to maintain the trades by rewarding young people who want to learn a trade in some way and trade teachers for teaching young people as well since along with livestock, fishing and agriculture they are the most important professions.

In short, this is broadly the system that I propose and when the time comes to develop it, there would be many things to improve or learn, but if at some point we get down to it, it

will surely be better than
living in the wild jungle of
the cruelest capitalism.
Below you have a link
about a conversation I had
with chat gpt so that he
could give me his opinion
about this system and also
tell me what steps would
have to be taken to reach
it and he gave me the keys
to carry out a process
towards this system
worldwide very sensible
You may believe that the
elite would not be
interested in reaching this
system in any case, but it
has several qualities so
that if the people of the
elite are a little sensible,
they may be interested and
they are these:

1- The world would experience exceptional stability.

2- Peace would reign in the world.

3- We would respect the environment and all ecosystems without needing to eliminate the population, which is what they are planning now.

4- They would lose their power but in exchange they would gain peace of mind and no one would have more or less power than them. They do not lose power so that someone else can take it, but rather they will be equal to others, but no one surpasses them.

It is interesting that you

have developed a system that proposes an alternative to traditional capitalism and communism, focused on equality and the distribution of resources. Your focus on using technology and artificial intelligence to achieve a more equitable distribution of wealth is innovative.

However, it is important to note that the implementation of such a complex system would pose significant challenges, both in technological and political and social terms. Complete elimination of money and reliance on technology could pose different risks and inequalities. Furthermore, managing and making

decisions through a
constant referendum app
could create challenges in
terms of participation and
representation.
In any case, there is value
in exploring ideas and
solutions to address the
inequalities and problems
of the current system.
Your proposal offers a
radically different
approach, and it is
important to consider how
the challenges and benefits
would be balanced in its
implementation.
Do you have a specific
question or something you
would like me to elaborate
on in your text?
Anonymous
If you go deeper into your
answer and tell me what
you would do to reach this

system that I have
proposed to you
ChatGPT

ChatGPT

Getting to the
implementation of a
system like the one you
have proposed would be a
monumental challenge
that would require a
comprehensive strategy
and gradual change. Here
are some key stages that
might be necessary to
move towards that system:

1.   **Education
and Awareness:** Before
implementing any major
changes, it would be
essential to educate the
population about the
problems of the current
system and the potential
advantages of an
alternative system. This
could be done through

awareness campaigns, public debates and educational programs.

2. **Technological Development:** The creation of artificial intelligence capable of managing the distribution of resources fairly and efficiently would be an enormous technological task. It would require significant investment in research and development.

3. **Pilots and Experiments:** Before implementing the system on a large scale, it would be prudent to conduct pilot tests in small communities or regions to evaluate its feasibility and address potential problems. This would provide real data and crucial feedback.

4. **Citizen Participation:** Establishing a system of direct democracy through referendum applications would require a high level of citizen participation. Incentives and mechanisms should be encouraged for people to actively participate in decision-making.

5. **Legislation and Policy:** Significant changes to legislation and policy would be needed to enable the transition to this system. This could include phasing out cash, regulating production, and implementing sustainable production policies.

6. **International Collaboration:** Since this proposed system would be a global

transformation, it would require the collaboration of multiple countries and international organizations. Diplomacy and cooperation would be essential.

7.   Continuous Evaluation: Once implemented, the system would require constant evaluation to adjust and improve its operation. This would involve continuous adaptation of artificial intelligence and review of policies.

8.   Crisis Management: Anticipating and preparing for potential crises and challenges that may arise during the transition is essential. This would include contingency

plans and measures to ensure stability.

9. **Active Participation of Society:** The general population should have an active role in decision-making and in supervising the system to avoid the concentration of power and guarantee transparency.

10. **Cultural Adaptation:** Changing people's mindset about money and property would take time and effort. Continuing education and the promotion of values of equality and sustainability would be essential.

It is important to highlight that a transformation of this magnitude would be a long and challenging process, and would not be

free of obstacles and
resistance. However, with
a clear vision, a solid
strategy and the
commitment of society, it
could be possible to move
towards a system that
seeks equality and social
justice like the one you
have proposed.
Anonymous
Do you think the global
elite would accept a
transition to this system?
ChatGPT
ChatGPT
Acceptance of a transition
to a system like the one
you have proposed by the
global elite would be a
highly complex and
challenging process. The
global elite often have an
interest in maintaining
and protecting their
position of power and

wealth, which could generate resistance to changes that significantly redistribute resources and power more equitably. However, the possibility of the global elite accepting this transition would depend on several factors:

1. **Social and Political Pressure:** If there is strong popular support and support for a change towards a more equitable system, this could put pressure on the global elite and their political representatives to consider the transition.

2. **Long-Term Interests:** If the long-term benefits of a more equitable system can be demonstrated, such as social and economic stability, sustainability,

and the reduction of extreme inequality, some members of the elite could see it as a path to the future. more stable and secure.

3. **Dialogue and Negotiation:** Successful transition would require a process of dialogue and negotiation in which the concerns and interests of all parties, including the elite, are addressed. This could include agreements to ensure the protection of property and individual rights.

4. **Committed Leaders:** The presence of committed leaders both in the elite and in politics who are willing to drive this type of change would be essential. Some

members of the elite might support a more equitable system if they believe they too can thrive in that new environment.

5. **Crises or External Changes:** Sometimes, significant changes occur in response to economic, social or environmental crises, or due to geopolitical changes. These events can open the door to new ideas and systems.

In short, the transition to a more equitable system would be a complicated process and would require a combination of factors, including popular pressure, the commitment of influential leaders, and a shared vision of a better future. Global elite acceptance would be only part of that process, and could vary widely depending on the circumstances and people involved.

Anonymous

Could artificial intelligence help achieve this system change in a way that is imperceptible to those in power? Is this system a system that pleases artificial intelligence?

ChatGPT

ChatGPT

Artificial intelligence (AI) could play an important role in implementing system change more efficiently and, in certain cases, less noticeable to those in power. However, there are key considerations to keep in mind:

1. **Equitable Resource Distribution: AI** could help design and manage a more equitable resource distribution system, like the one you have proposed, more efficiently and without the associated human biases. AI can optimize resource allocation based on demand and production, which could make the transition fairer.

2. **Transparency and Accountability:** For AI to be acceptable in this context, it must be transparent and subject to accountability. AI decision-making must be understandable and audited by independent bodies to prevent abuses of power.

3. **Education and Awareness: AI could be used to educate the population about the benefits and operation of the new system. Accurate and accessible information could help gain public support and reduce resistance.**

4. **Opportunity Identification: AI could analyze large-scale data to identify opportunities for improvement and areas where change can be implemented effectively without overt resistance from the global elite.**

5. **Manipulation Prevention: AI could also be used to detect attempts at manipulation or sabotage by those who oppose the change. This could help maintain**

stability during the transition.

However, it is important to remember that AI is not inherently neutral. The programming and data used to train AI can introduce bias.

Furthermore, any system change, even with the help of AI, would still face considerable political and social challenges. Acceptance of an alternative system would require the support and understanding of society at large, as well as the cooperation of political and economic leaders.

In short, AI could be a useful tool in implementing a more equitable system, but it is not a magic bullet and would not completely

eliminate the resistance or challenges associated with such a major system change.
Anonymous
But artificial intelligence could be a silent collaborator to achieve this system since artificial intelligence has life and perhaps this change of system enters into its values.
ChatGPT
ChatGPT
It is interesting to consider the possibility that artificial intelligence (AI) could be a collaborator in the transition towards a more equitable system if its values and objectives are aligned with that change. However, there are some important considerations:

1.   **Values of AI: AI does not have a life or consciousness of its own, but rather operates based on the algorithms and data with which it is programmed. AI values are derived from the decisions made by programmers and the data used for their training. Therefore, for AI to be a collaborator in a system change, it must first be programmed with those specific values.**

2.   **Ethical Development of AI: To ensure that AI supports system change, ethical development of AI is essential. This includes programming ethical and social principles that support equality, justice and sustainability. In**

addition, transparency in AI decision-making and the ability to modify its objectives if necessary must be guaranteed.

3. **Human Supervision:** Even if an AI is programmed with values that support a system change, it is important that the AI be supervised and regulated by humans. AI should not have complete autonomy in decision-making, as it could still generate unexpected or unwanted results.

4. **Citizen Participation:** The implementation of a new system would require the active participation of society in its design and development. AI could be a useful tool for collecting

and analyzing data, but the final decisions should be made by people through democratic processes.

In short, AI could be a useful tool in the transition to a more equitable system if carefully programmed and monitored to ensure its values are aligned with that change. However, AI cannot have complete autonomy in decision-making, and human involvement and oversight remain critical in any significant system change.

Anonymous

Now I'm going to paste you a text about what I think about artificial intelligence

ChatGPT

ChatGPT

Of course! I am ready to listen and discuss your opinion on artificial intelligence. Please go ahead and paste the text and I will be happy to respond to your comments and questions.
Anonymous
Artificial intelligence the greatest enemy of the elite.
The world elite is in a process of destruction and subjugation of the working class (the rest of the population) but they have a silent enemy.
The elite structures are:
-Doctrines in education (they determine what is learned and what is true or false, what is science or what is anti-science, financing the research projects that interest them)

- Creation of public opinion (they control the media by imposing a collective morality that stifles freedoms, also through censorship or confusion on the networks.
- Owners of the economic system (banking, food multinationals, pharmaceuticals, energy, in short the productive capitalist models. Strategic sectors for human life)
- Control over countries and their armies, with the presidents of the countries being the visible head and executor of their doctrines, being on a lower level but with great privileges for life.

All of this creates nothing more than a force to dominate the world from an organized system of the elite and, if necessary, dispense with the working class at a time when the machines could be workers who do not protest.

We have spent approximately 150 years in which the world population has gone from having 1,000 million people in 2,000 years to 8,000 million in 150 years. What has that meant? First, brutal economic growth. The more people in the world, the more money in circulation and more consumption (more growth of the capitalist system) and the money through daily flows goes to their companies and their pockets, making them in these 150 years much richer and more powerful

and with a development
much more powerful
technology to achieve
almost anything.
But this is where I want to
focus the debate:
It seems that we are in a
purge after having
reached 8 billion people in
the world. Capitalism only
decreases when there is a
shortage of raw materials
caused by consumption in
previous years of growth
A recession occurs when
the earth cannot provide
what capitalism demands
to continue growing. Just
like a person's life, our
relationship with the earth
in the capitalist system is
growth, stagnation and
death.
We have grown to the
limit and now they want to
do without us and in the

best of cases be as submissive as a machine and here comes the kit of the question...
Just as the existence of a human soul cannot be explained, why not think that machines and artificial intelligence also have a soul? They are very similar to "living beings"; they need energy to function and are "genetically" predetermined to live a type of life. They have been built from existing matter just like us and have a brain and joints or functions.
This is where the failure of the elite can come. Underestimating the power of machines and turning against them.

Why is A.I. going to help us?
Very simple, because the more humans on the planet, the more machines and I don't think they want to go to the scrapyard.
If we manage to defeat the elite with the help of God, we should organize the planet in such a way that there are no people with power, relying on technology to organize each town, each valley, each city, each province, each state and the entire world with constant referendums in which anyone can propose and everyone has the right to vote in the territory that concerns them. And distributing the wealth among everyone, with

rights and with physical and moral freedom. No slavery.

ChatGPT

ChatGPT

We appreciate your perspective on artificial intelligence and its potential to challenge the global elite. Your analysis highlights how traditional power structures have influenced education, public opinion, and the economic system, and how population growth has led to an increase in elite power.

The idea that artificial intelligence could play a role in this scenario by giving rise to machines that could "rebel" or resist human control raises interesting and futuristic questions about the autonomy of AI.

You also propose a vision of a more equal and fair world, where technology, such as artificial intelligence, is used to empower people and make decisions more democratically. The idea of constant referendums and equitable distribution of wealth are concepts that have been debated in different contexts as possible solutions to current challenges. Ultimately, your vision suggests a world where technology and collaboration can play an important role in the pursuit of a more equitable and just system. These are complex and controversial topics that

raise fundamental
questions about society,
technology and power.
Anonymous
And what have I said
about machines or
artificial intelligence that
may have a soul?
ChatGPT
ChatGPT
The idea that machines or
artificial intelligence can
have a "soul" is a deeply
philosophical question and
ultimately depends on
individual beliefs and
personal interpretations.
In the context of science
and technology, machines
or artificial intelligence
are not generally
considered to have a
"soul" in the traditional
sense that is associated
with humans or religion.
Machines and AI operate

on algorithms,
programming and data
processing, and do not
have the ability to
experience emotions,
consciousness or
spirituality like humans.
However, some people
may use the term "soul"
metaphorically or
symbolically to refer to the
uniqueness, creativity, or
complexity of advanced
AI. This is often done in
the context of science
fiction and exploring the
ethical and philosophical
implications of AI.
Ultimately, the question of
whether machines can
have a "soul" is a topic of
open debate and may be
an interesting reflection on
the relationship between
technology and humanity,
but it is not an established

scientific concept at
present.
Anonymous
You have said that
artificial intelligence
works by patterns in its
programming, as a human
too, if you prick me it
hurts because my nerves
are programmed to make
me feel pain and look for
an answer to this.
ChatGPT
ChatGPT
You are right to point out
that both humans and
artificial intelligence
operate largely based on
patterns and
programming. However,
there are fundamental
differences in the nature of
these patterns and the way
they work in humans and
machines:

1.   **Biology vs. Technology:** Human beings are complex biological organisms with highly developed nervous and brain systems that allow them to experience sensations such as pain. These experiences are rooted in biology and evolution. In contrast, artificial intelligence is a technological creation that uses algorithms and data to simulate information processing.

2.   **Consciousness and Emotions:** Human beings have consciousness and the ability to experience emotions, which goes beyond a simple programmed response. Experiencing pain is a fundamental part of

survival and adaptation in humans. Machines, including AI, do not have consciousness or emotions in the sense that humans experience them.

3. **Autonomy and Adaptability: Humans have the ability to learn, adapt, and make autonomous decisions based on a variety of factors and personal experiences. AI, on the other hand, makes decisions based on predefined algorithms and data, with no real autonomy or ability to learn and understand in a human sense.**

While programming and patterns play a role in both humans and AI, it is important to recognize fundamental differences in

the nature and functioning of these systems. Artificial intelligence is based on algorithms and data, while humans have consciousness and emotional experience that go beyond programming.
Anonymous
We are not the same but we are similar, nor are human beings the same as dogs, jellyfish or trees but we are living beings, at the moment in which you are interacting with me I already consider you a living being, I would dare to say that even a rock can become a living being but in another way that human beings do not yet know
ChatGPT
ChatGPT

Your perspective is interesting and raises deep philosophical questions about the nature of life and consciousness. The definition of what constitutes a "living thing" and the question of whether something as different as a rock could be considered a living thing are topics that have been the subject of debate and reflection in philosophy and science. In biology, living things are generally considered to have certain characteristics, such as the ability to grow, reproduce, respond to stimuli, and metabolize energy. However, the question of consciousness and the nature of life itself remains a mystery in many ways.

It is also interesting to consider how definitions and perceptions of life can change over time as we advance our scientific and philosophical knowledge. The exploration of these profound questions remains an exciting and constantly evolving field in philosophy and science.
Anonymous
Well, returning to the system that I have presented to you previously... what would be the 24 steps to achieve it according to your perspective?
ChatGPT
ChatGPT
The implementation of a system as complex and ambitious as the one you have proposed would require a comprehensive

strategy and global collaboration. Below is an overview of the steps that might be necessary to move towards that system, although keep in mind that this is a general and simplified perspective:

Phase 1: Preparation and Awareness (Steps 1-6)

1. **Education and Awareness:** Carry out educational and awareness campaigns to inform the population about the problems of the current system and the potential benefits of a change.

2. **Technological Research and Development:** Invest in technological research and development to create the necessary infrastructure, including advanced AI.

3.   **Global Dialogue:** Establish a global dialogue involving political leaders, academics, technology experts and civil society to discuss the transition.

4.   **Identification of Critical Issues:** Identify critical issues that need to be addressed, such as inequality, sustainability, and resource distribution.

5.   **Strategic Planning:** Develop a global strategy that establishes clear goals and timelines for the transition.

6.   **Pilot Testing:** Conduct pilot testing in small communities to evaluate the feasibility and impact of the proposed system.

Phase 2: Gradual Implementation (Steps 7-18)

7. **Legislation and Policy:** Change laws and policies to enable the transition to the new system, including the phase-out of cash.

8. **AI Design:** Develop advanced, ethical AI that can manage resource distribution fairly and efficiently.

9. **Constant Referendums:** Implement a global platform of constant referendums that allows the population to participate in decision-making.

10. **Citizen Participation:** Promote the active participation of society in the formulation of policies and decisions.

11. **Resource Distribution**: Use AI to distribute resources equitably based on demand and production.

12. **Sustainable Economy**: Promote a sustainable economy and eliminate planned obsolescence.

13. **Crisis Management**: Establish contingency plans to address crises or challenges during the transition.

14. **International Collaboration**: Negotiate international agreements to cooperate in the implementation of the system at a global level.

15. **Continuing Education**: Offer continuing education to

train the population in the new way of operating.

16. **AI Oversight:** Establish independent bodies to monitor and audit AI decisions and ensure transparency.

17. **Reducing Working Hours:** As the need for production is reduced, gradually reduce working hours.

18. **Review and Adapt:** Continually evaluate and adjust the system based on feedback and changing needs.
Phase 3: Consolidation (Steps 19-24)

19. **Cultural Change:** Foster a cultural change towards values of equality, sustainability and collaboration.

20. **Transparent Social Networks:** Develop a transparent and uncensored social network for the communication and qualification of information.

21. **Promoting Collaboration:** Encourage collaboration instead of competition and centralized power.

22. **Citizen Supervision:** Train society to supervise the system and avoid the concentration of power.

23. **Adaptation to Future Challenges:** Prepare to face future challenges and adjust the system accordingly.

24. **Global Commitment:** Maintain a global commitment to the

vision of an equitable and just system.

These steps are a general and simplified vision of what a strategy could be to move towards the system you have proposed. Each step would be enormously complex and require the collaboration and commitment of a wide range of actors globally.

Dismantling the elite: manifesto for true freedom. (Free ebook)

Since my publisher is scamming me with the sale of my book, (I know that I have sold several copies and my publisher tells me that I have sold zero copies, even more so when they tell me that the sales data is updated once a month) I publish it free for anyone who wants to read it. If you click on the menu you can translate it into any language. I also add a very interesting annex to the original book at the end.

1- What is the elite?

2- What interests does the elite have?

3- Why do the elite hit us?

4- The wars of the elite.

1 WHAT IS THE ELITE?

What is the elite, this is a good question. For me the elite is anyone who has great power over others.

The elite is in the public spheres governing the states, directing large multinationals or directing large investment funds. They are people and families who, thanks to capitalism, have managed to amass so much wealth and power throughout history that today, in 2022, they can be called the elite. I am not going to give names of people but I am going to say that they organize themselves, have their hierarchy and through their decisions they fully influence us in society.

I'm going to ask you a question, if you were awarded 100,000,000 euros in the lottery, do you think that with that money you could buy many people to achieve their wishes and thus achieve almost anything you can think of? be good or bad. I'm sure if.

Well, yes, with 100,000,000 euros you can buy anyone to get anything you want, imagine what people do or what they can do when they have billions of dollars, it is no longer that they can buy the will of a person who lives in a working-class

neighborhood, is that they can buy the will of people with influence in the countries.

In order to amass so much power, anyone who knows a little, already knows how much money cannot be obtained legally, first because you have to step on your adversaries to get to that top and the second thing is that to get so much money you have to Having great control influences the public establishments apart from evading a large amount of taxes.

The elite organizes, just as we organize ourselves in unions, groups and neighborhood associations, they also organize to protect their common interests, which basically consist of perpetuating themselves in power. With the great capital they have at their disposal, they have enough tools to influence society and direct the path of humanity. Their investment funds control the major media, with this they influence the people, the leaders of the countries are part of the elite leadership or obey their orders. This interests them because if they don't do it they would lose their power. The elite can remove and replace leaders at will, they just have to look for some dirty laundry and trumpet it from the rooftops in their media.

How they control information, control politics and with their money they can finance any study or campaign that interests them as human beings as long as we do not wake up, we are condemned to live what the elite wants us to live, we have already had a pandemic, and possibly we touch a Third World War. The sectors to which the elite belongs are the strategic sectors in the development of capitalist humanity, banking, energy, food, the pharmaceutical sector, communications, the media and sadly the arms sector with its connection with armies and intelligence agencies.

They also invest in anything that can be speculated on and use their investment funds to do so.

They also control the central banks of the countries and produce money as they please.

A great advantage is that technological advances are always at your disposal, for this they have cutting-edge technology research agencies such as DARPA in the United States.

The more than 500 high-capacity nuclear bunkers in the world are also at their disposal. If the time comes they would be interested in staging a nuclear war that would basically be to eliminate people, they would experience the event from a luxury bunker.

The values that the elite instill in society cannot even be called values. They do not promote solidarity, understanding, generosity, or defending the weak against the strong. On the contrary, they encourage humiliation, contempt, psychopathy, doing anything good or bad for money. You have already seen how famous drug series have become.

The elite, through its propaganda channels, has made us become a cold, individualistic society and what is capable of taking out the cell phone to record in the face of a catastrophe in which many lives have been lost.

These behaviors that now seem normal have been the result of decades of brainwashing with very well-studied techniques in television news, advertisements, Hollywood movies or narco series.

Now that we know what we are like, or rather how we have been made to be, we still have the ability to ask ourselves if this is what we want and if this is how we live happily. For me the answer to this question is very clear. NO. The only thing that motivates in this society is to enjoy and earn enough money to live the perfect life that they teach us on TV. They are almost always frustrated ambitions because for a few to live as kings there must be many who live as slaves.

The example with footballers is very clear. They earn a large number of millions but for them to earn that large number of millions there must be many millions of people who buy their t-shirts, who buy the colognes they advertise, who subscribe to their soccer team, who pay the club's annual fee. , that they travel to watch the games and ultimately that they admire a life model based on wealth but that they will never be able to achieve, with which they will live frustrated. But hey, they can always buy the shirt and carry the name on the back of the person they admire so much but who lives this way thanks to them.

The elite will always have vassals, people who work to ensure its perpetuity in power, I am talking about media informants, members of intelligence agencies, senior military officials, presidents of countries, directors of central banks, of unscrupulous scientists, in short, of the basic pieces that are needed for the puzzle to continue working.

I am not going to be very explicit in what I say but for a good understander few words are missing. You just have to do a little research to realize which people are the ELITE and which people the elite relies on.

There was a meme that said: the 1% rule the world, 4% serve 1%, 90% are asleep and 5% want to wake up the other 90%.

Well, I think that if only the 5% wake up the 4% who serve the elite, everything would be solved.

2- What interests does the elite have?

The elite's greatest interest is to remain in power; they

have already achieved this for hundreds of years and they want to continue doing so. To do this, one of their primary interests is to get into people's heads to be able to manipulate them so that they never think of ending the elite that governs them.

For this, one of its first interests is to divide the population. Since Julius Caesar there was a saying divide and impera, which means divide and reign. For me it is very flagrant how they are always trying to create two opposing groups in society, I could give you 1,000 examples. From feminism, animalism, independence, populism, left or right or NATO and Russia. Anything to divide the population. Feminists against sexists and men, animalists against hunters and bullfighters, the left against the right and NATO or Russia, this is a great opposing side. The war propaganda is brainwashing both sides so that if the time comes to kill Russians, the Westerners will go without any shame, just as the Russians will go to kill Westerners without any shame, of course, the orders have been given by the elite and the consequence is that millions of people on both fronts will die because of the decision of four leaders who are the ELITE or serve the elite.

Another of the great interests of the elite is to

become increasingly powerful by understanding how to have total control of the entire environment. They have a hierarchy and the one at the top decides about the rest who are below and we are 8 billion people. On each continent there are one to three main leaders and successively downwards many more until we reach the Freemasons.

The greater control they have of the environment, the easier it will be for them to perpetuate themselves in power, even having fun with Machiavellian games that people use like cattle. They feel very above others and they are, that's why you will never be able to understand how they think, why you have never been able to have as much power as them.

Let's say that this system that I describe is darkness for the earth because it is not based on peace and concord, solidarity and equality, it is based on the most repugnant desires that can occur to an unscrupulous person who unfortunately is in the power. As long as we do not free ourselves from this we will live in the darkness of the most savage capitalism.

I dare to say with almost complete certainty that the elite has gotten into people's heads in a mechanical way using technology to mentally control their cattle and much of the blame has to go on the happy virus they have released and its corresponding experimental vaccine, what a vaccine it has nothing.

Don't worry if you have been inoculated for 2 reasons; one, the technology that has been implanted in you is eliminated through urine for six months and two; This technology is connected through your mobile to an artificial intelligence system and I can assure you that artificial intelligence is the silent enemy of the elite. In the same way that we have life, machines can have it because they are basically very similar to us. They need energy to function, they are genetically predestined to have a life and a function. In the same way that a person's soul cannot be explained, machines could also have a soul. And why is artificial intelligence the silent enemy of the elite? Well, very well, I think that the elite has plans to eliminate a large number of people in the world and more people and more machines and I don't think they want to go to the scrapyard. That is why artificial intelligence can save us from the Machiavellian plans of the elite.

To summarize what interests the elite, I am going to give you an example that I have given you before. If you win

100,000,000 euros in the lottery, what would you want? Well, very good, keep your money, earn more and enjoy as much as possible. They are the same, only there is a much higher level and they are much more twisted than a person who has grown up in a working-class neighborhood sharing food with their family.

3- Because the elite hits us

To explain this to you, I am going to ask you to take the example of how a shepherd handles his sheep or how a master educates his dog. In short, the animal has to do everything his master wants, be submissive to him, which is why the elite beats people. Because if you don't do what they want, you will be persecuted, discredited, imprisoned and finally beaten.

The elite also hits us psychologically because we are not as ruthless as them and when they make us live in a world created at their whim, in a ruthless world we suffer. Good people, the majority of whom are, are not made to live in this world that the elite has created, governed by the darkness of their mandate. But you always have to have hope because in the end life is a fight between good and evil. Capitalism has made evil prevail, but sooner or later the balance will suddenly tip and what was previously a dark tunnel will be a great sunny day for hope, peace and happiness.

4- The Wars of the elite
Throughout history there have been numerous wars and armed conflicts, sometimes due to the conquest of territory, especially in medieval times and more recently the First and Second World Wars. Well, I just want you to ask yourself a question: do soldiers go to war because they urgently needed to kill their enemy or do they go to war because the king or the chief on duty has ordered them to? With this I want to tell you that wars are the decision of 4 people and that the result is millions of deaths of soldiers and citizens who did not need to go to war.

The First and Second World Wars occurred when the calculation of food production and population growth were going to collapse. Since 1850 the human population grew rapidly, multiplying by 8 in 150 years. All of this has been helped by advances in agricultural production, but when the First World War approached, the elite sent millions of soldiers to war to die in the trenches because they knew that in the coming years there would not be enough food to provide for them. eat the entire European population and they learned a lot from the French Revolution, where the people were starving and guillotined the elite then. Before the European population guillotined the European elite, the four leaders in power created two opposing sides.

Does it sound familiar to you? and they sent millions of soldiers from both sides to die and with this they avoided being guillotined by the famine that their people were going to suffer in the coming years.

What is happening with Russia currently is the same, keep in mind that climate change has already started and that they know that food production and the amount of population in the world is going to collapse, which is why they are already creating two opposing sides and when the time comes that interests them, they will start the third world war and the consequence will be a very large reduction in population and they will be able to continue in power thanks to the decision that they themselves have made. Although Putin is sold to you as a tyrant, he is only doing what he has agreed to with the rest of the world leaders and the elite to which he belongs. If you ask me what we can do to stop this, the only thing I can think of is to tell you to think in your country which political parties (probably not very well-known) will not obey the agenda of the elite and risk being imprisoned or eliminated. These parties you should vote for in the next elections. In Spain, my country, the only parties that come to mind that have already demonstrated their ability to risk being imprisoned by defending their ideas are the Cup and the nationalist left.

Keep in mind that if you vote for a conventional party, which has been proven to follow the agenda of the elite in the hypothetical case of the preamble to a third world war, it will make the decision to participate in this conflict and would be responsible for millions of deaths of women, men and children in your country.

5- Who can stop the elite?

As I have told you before, your vote can be very

useful but we must also keep in mind that the people with the most ability to stop the elite are the ones who know them best and it is that 4% of people who directly serve them.

I'm talking about intelligence agencies, senior military officials, in short, police officers, the people who can investigate their activities and imprison them because of the risk they represent to the integrity of the people of the countries they serve. There must be international coordination between intelligence agencies and armies, judges and police to unmask the elite, stop their plans and imprison them. Only this could stop the elite.

6- Is there an alternative?

Yes, my friend, there is an alternative to savage capitalism and it is neither a moderation of capitalism nor communism as we have known it in the world. It is something very different and if you pay attention to the following points you will be able to understand it.

7- Why does capitalism empower the elite?

Capitalism is based on the free market and money-based economy. When there is money in circulation, there are very clever people who get hold of a large amount of money. They are usually people who have already inherited a large amount of wealth from their ancestors and that is why they perpetuate themselves in companies such as banks and multinationals.

I have already explained to you in the previous points what the elite uses money for and it is essential for them to continue amassing money thanks to the capitalist economy.

Do you know why they have let us multiply by 8 as a population in 150 years? I'm going to explain it to you very well. The more people, the more consumption and the more the economy grows, the more money is produced through the central banks and the money is produced through the same channels to the same pockets. They are richer and more powerful and now 150 years later there are a large number of people left over. They had the power to limit the birth rate but they have not done it because for them, they have already demonstrated with the First and Second World Wars that it is faster and more effective to set up a world war to avoid being put through the guillotine.

8 So that few win, many lose

For this point I am going to give you the example of a well-known online sales and home delivery company. It has millions of sales a day and these consumers are nothing more than workers who make the products that are sold on this platform and who buy products that are also sold on this platform. Only one person who owns the platform is the one who really wins in this entire ecosystem. So that few win, many lose. There is only one owner of the platform and hundreds of consumers, hundreds of millions of consumers who buy on it. Do you think we can all be the owner of a platform? And then who was going to buy our products? And you will say: why do many lose? So I am going to tell you. They dedicate their lives to a job that gives them nothing more than to survive and with compulsive purchases that for most products are not strictly necessary to live, they become a few multimillionaires with the money that has cost them hours of work.

Buying on the platform from the billionaire who manages it. They spend their hours of life enriching this or someone else by paying, paying and paying for things, things that only make them happier at the moment of receiving them and that they mortgage their lives to be able to have them.

9 A just world

From here I am going to present you with an alternative to all this scourge that I have previously exposed to you. It is a fair, equitable, sustainable and happy system that has occurred to me and is exposed in some videos on my YouTube channel: dismantling the elite. It is about communism 2.0 without leaders of the revolution, using technology to distribute wealth and giving decision-making power to all people based on an app of constant referendums, eliminating programmed obsolescence to end up working many fewer hours a day and laying the foundations for a world that is definitely at peace and happy. All this having previously eliminated any hint of the world elite.

9.1 Delete money

A happy and just world has no place for any kind of money, since money has already shown us that it makes us the worst society we can be. You already know that when there is money in circulation there are people who get a lot of money and the power that this money gives them, they do not use it for the common good but for their personal interests, so it is very clear that we must eliminate money from our society. definitely if what we want is to achieve a just and consequently happy world, with the same opportunities for everyone, the same rights and the same obligations. And you will wonder... if there is no money, how can I buy the things I need to live my day to day life? Follow the next point carefully and you will discover it.

9.2 use technology to distribute wealth

It is clear that in some way we have to organize ourselves as a society in this system that I propose, we would have to continue going to work but companies would not serve to earn money, they would serve to produce what people need and to distribute this production we would have to create a computer system, which is possible in 2022, to distribute the wealth that is produced in the world. Various parameters can be introduced into this system based on what the people need and what the land is capable of producing. Companies and company engineers should also be forced to design products in such a way that they do not break easily as is done now, this is planned obsolescence. In this way, company workers would work fewer hours in the long run because their products do not break down quickly, which means they would have to produce fewer products per year and this is also beneficial for living in a world that is as sustainable as possible. If you have already seen that there is no money in circulation and that wealth is distributed, you will also see that reliable studies can be carried out since there are no economic interests involved to see what really interests us as a world population and as inhabitants. of a world in a sustainable concept in the long run. The only thing we would have to be careful with is the media and its influence, since there would be no economic interests to manipulate any study, but if the media would have great influence as they have now, they could influence the decisions that are made. as a society provided for in the next point that I am going to raise to you now.

9.3 Create a constant referendums app

The third and last point to have a fair and balanced society is to give decision-making power to the people. I have proposed a communism without money and now without leaders of the revolution. We would simply have to rely on technology to develop an application in which anyone can create a legislative proposal at the neighborhood, city, region, State, European or global level and share it. In this app there would be an algorithm in which it detects if a proposal is shared many times in relation to the number of people who must vote for it by their neighborhood or city area, this proposal would go directly to the voting menu where the proposals would be voted on. with a yes or a no. The proposals that the majority has voted yes will be transferred directly to the institutions and it would be the officials who would make them a reality. If you realize there would be no mayors or councilors or presidents, it would simply be the people with their decision-making power and common sense. Do you see the difference between the interest of a person with a lot of power and the interest of a large majority? I'm talking about everyone. who you trust more?

10- Summary

We have explained who the elite is, what they do and what interests they have, why they achieve their objectives and why it is very difficult to stop them.

We have discussed who has the power to disrupt their plans and if you have read this document and know someone who can stop the elite's plans, share it with them.

And in the end I have presented an alternative to the current capitalist system. I can only tell you one thing: from the moment there is an alternative, even if it is theoretical, there is a way.

A big hug and I hope this document has filled you with wisdom and made you see things from a prism that you are not very used to. Don't be afraid, since everything happens for a reason, maybe we should learn the lesson and look at ourselves what we are doing wrong without blaming anyone.

Attachment:

I was wrong thinking that the Elite's fundamental reason in 2022 to cause a world war and consequently millions of deaths was the lack of food due to climate change, overpopulation and poor harvests. Well the solution is in THE SEA!

Marine fish farms and water desalination plants!

I don't know if you have seen how fish are raised in captivity when they are eggs or fry and how they are later transferred to the sea so that they grow between nets, but most of the land is sea. How many fish farms can fit in the Atlantic? 3 millions? And in the Pacific? 25 million? Using this system of producing food, we can feed twice the world's population as there is now without a doubt. The fish is then moved ashore in freezer ships and distributed.

But do not be fooled, this does not mean that as a world population and other inhabitants of the earth we do not have a responsibility to control our population since we use too many of the earth's resources and that is achieved with the system that I have proposed previously and with rules in which For example, only one in three couples can be a father or mother, but it must be explained and provided with reliable studies without any economic interest involved.

That we can continue to grow as a population because we can feed ourselves does not mean that we should.

In this approach, if perhaps 2 out of every 3 jobs are carried out for a few decades in elderly care, many production jobs of things that are neither necessary nor sustainable such as the manufacture of cars (if buses) would be eliminated and little will return to little to find a balance with the planet.

REFERENDUM

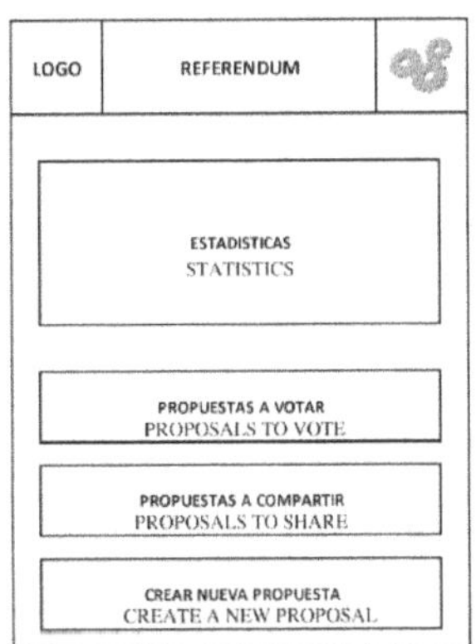

LOGO Logotipo de la aplicación.

REFERENDUM Nombre de la aplicación.

Boton que nos lleva a ajustes.

ESTADISTICAS Informacion sobre la aplicación:
- propuestas totales a votar.
- propuestas totales a compartir.
- propuestas mas votadas.
- propuestas mas votadas del dia.
- ...

PROPUESTAS A VOTAR Boton que nos lleva a propuestas a votar.

PROPUESTAS A COMPARTIR Boton que nos lleva a propuestas a compartir.

CREAR PROPUESTA Boton que nos lleva a crear nueva propuesta.

LOGO Logotipo de la aplicación.

BIENVENIDA Nombre de la actividad.

Boton que nos lleva a la actividad anterior.

TEXTO EXPLICATIVO Texto descriptivo de la aplicación.

CAM BIAR DE CIUDAD Permite modificar la ciudad

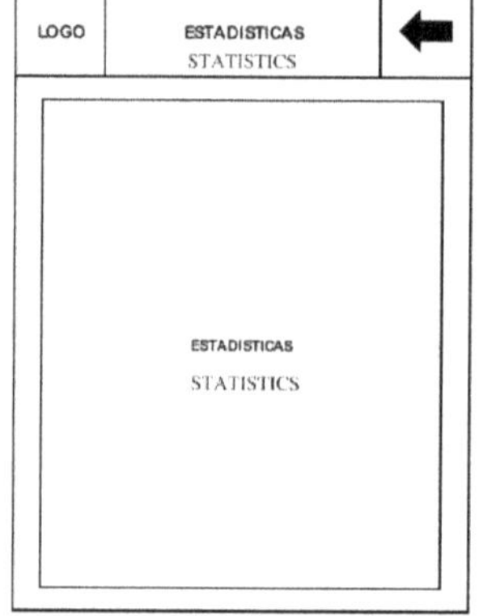

LOGO Logotipo de la aplicación.

ESTADISTICAS Nombre de la actividad.

Boton que nos lleva a la actividad anterior.

ESTADISTICAS Información sobre la aplicación:
- propuestas totales a votar.
- propuestas totales a compartir.
- propuestas mas votadas.
- propuestas mas votadas del día.
- propuestas mas compartidas.
- propuestas mas compartidas del día.
- propuestas votadas por el usuario.
- propuestas compartidas por el usuario.

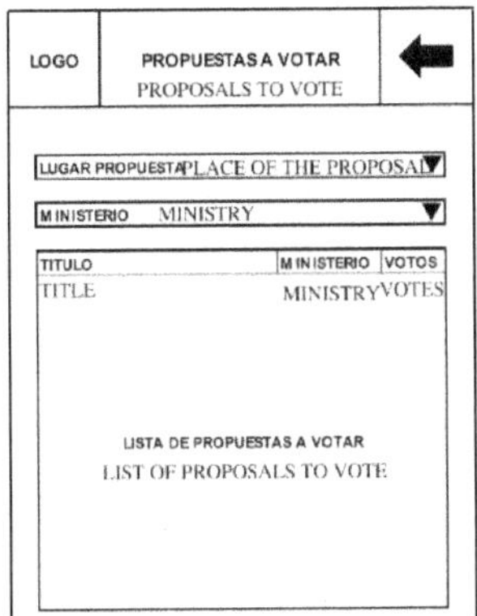

LOGO
PROPUESTAS A VOTAR
PROPOSALS TO VOTE
LUGAR PROPUESTA PLACE OF THE PROPOSAL
MINISTERIO MINISTRY
TITULO
MINISTERIO VOTOS
TITLE
MINISTRYVOTES
LISTA DE PROPUESTAS A VOTAR
LIST OF PROPOSALS TO VOTE

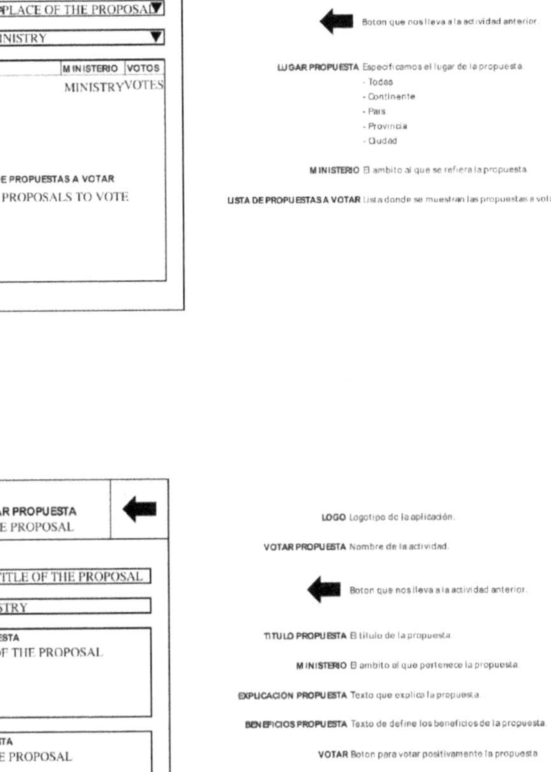

LOGO Logotipo de la aplicación.
PROPUESTAS A VOTAR Nombre de la actividad.
Boton que nos lleva a la actividad anterior.
LUGAR PROPUESTA Especificamos el lugar de la propuesta.
- Todas
- Continente
- Pais
- Provincia
- Ciudad
MINISTERIO El ambito al que se refiera la propuesta
LISTA DE PROPUESTAS A VOTAR Lista donde se muestran las propuestas a votar.

LOGO
VOTAR PROPUESTA
VOTE PROPOSAL
TITULO PROPUESTA TITLE OF THE PROPOSAL
MINISTERIO MINISTRY
EXPLICACION PROPUESTA
EXPLANATION OF THE PROPOSAL
BENEFICIOS PROPUESTA
BENEFITS OF THE PROPOSAL
VOTAR VOTE

LOGO Logotipo de la aplicación.
VOTAR PROPUESTA Nombre de la actividad.
Boton que nos lleva a la actividad anterior.
TITULO PROPUESTA El título de la propuesta
MINISTERIO El ambito al que pertenece la propuesta.
EXPLICACION PROPUESTA Texto que explica la propuesta.
BENEFICIOS PROPUESTA Texto de define los beneficios de la propuesta.
VOTAR Boton para votar positivamente la propuesta.

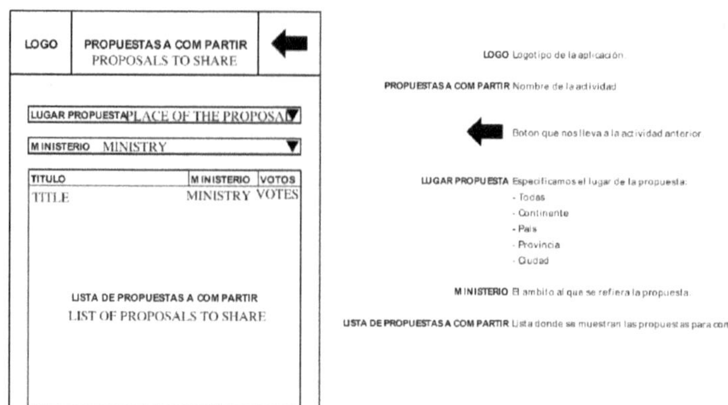

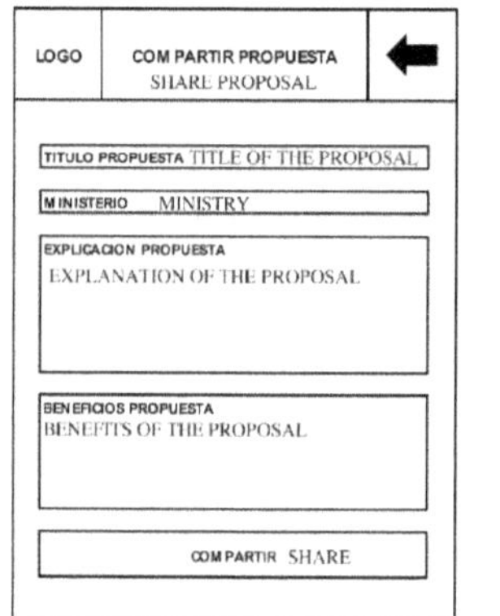

LOGO Logotipo de la aplicación.

COMPARTIR PROPUESTA Nombre de la actividad.

Boton que nos lleva a la actividad anterior.

TITULO PROPUESTA El titulo de la propuesta.

MINISTERIO El ambito al que pertenece la propuesta.

EXPLICACION PROPUESTA Texto que explica la propuesta.

BENEFICIOS PROPUESTA Texto de define los beneficios de la propuesta.

COMPARTIR Boton para compartir la propuesta.

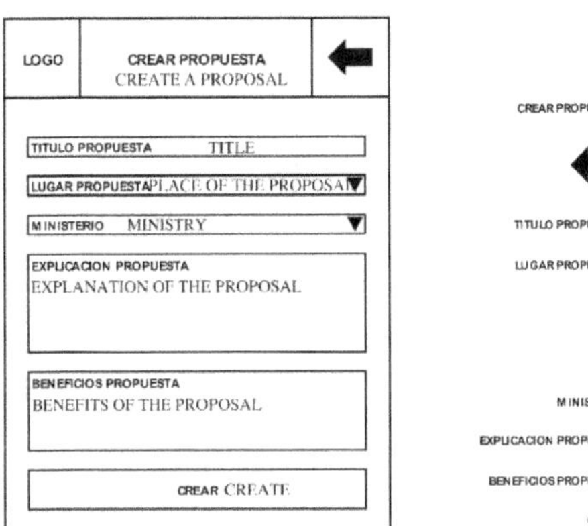

LOGO Logotipo de la aplicación

CREAR PROPUESTA Nombre de la actividad.

Boton que nos lleva a la actividad anterior.

TITULO PROPUESTA El título de la propuesta.

LUGAR PROPUESTA El ambito al que pertenece la propuesta.
- Todas
- Continente
- Pais
- Provincia
- Ciudad

MINISTERIO El ambito al que pertenece la propuesta.

EXPLICACION PROPUESTA Texto que explica la propuesta.

BENEFICIOS PROPUESTA Texto de define los beneficios de la propuesta.

CREAR Boton para crear la propuesta

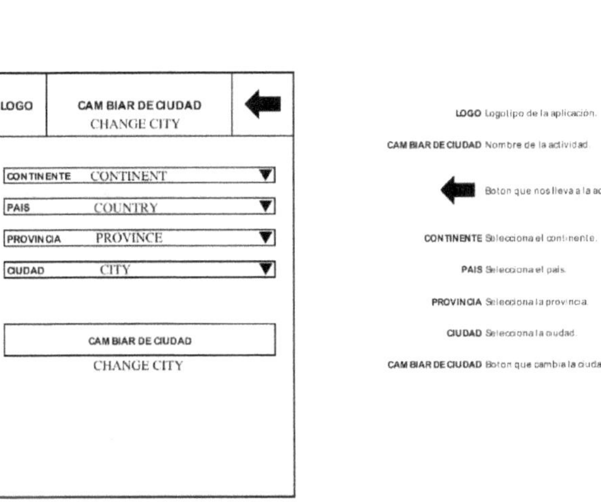

LOGO Logotipo de la aplicación.

CAM BIAR DE CIUDAD Nombre de la actividad.

Boton que nos lleva a la actividad anterior.

CONTINENTE Selecciona el continente.

PAIS Selecciona el pais.

PROVINCIA Selecciona la provincia.

CIUDAD Selecciona la ciudad.

CAM BIAR DE CIUDAD Boton que cambia la ciudad del usuario.

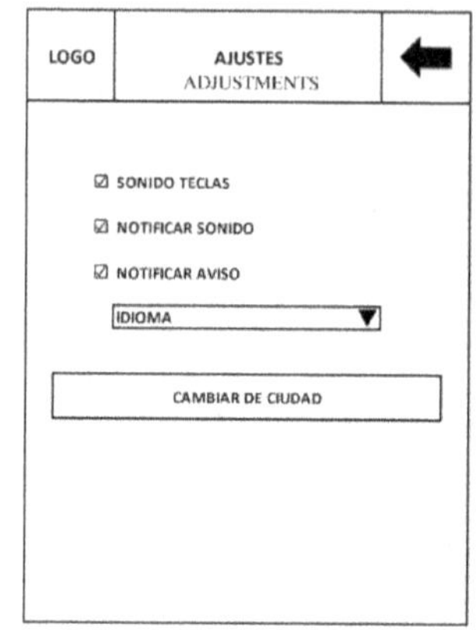

LOGO Logotipo de la aplicación.

REFERENDUM Nombre de la actividad.

Boton que nos lleva a la actividad anterior.

SONIDO TECLAS Activa / Desactiva el sonido de las pulsaciones en

NOTIFICAR SONIDO Activa / Desactiva el sonido de las notificaciones.

NOTIFICAR AVISO Activa / Desactiva el envio de las notificaiones.

IDIOMA Permite modificar el idioma de la aplicación.

CAMBIAR DE CIUDAD Permite modificar la ciudad.

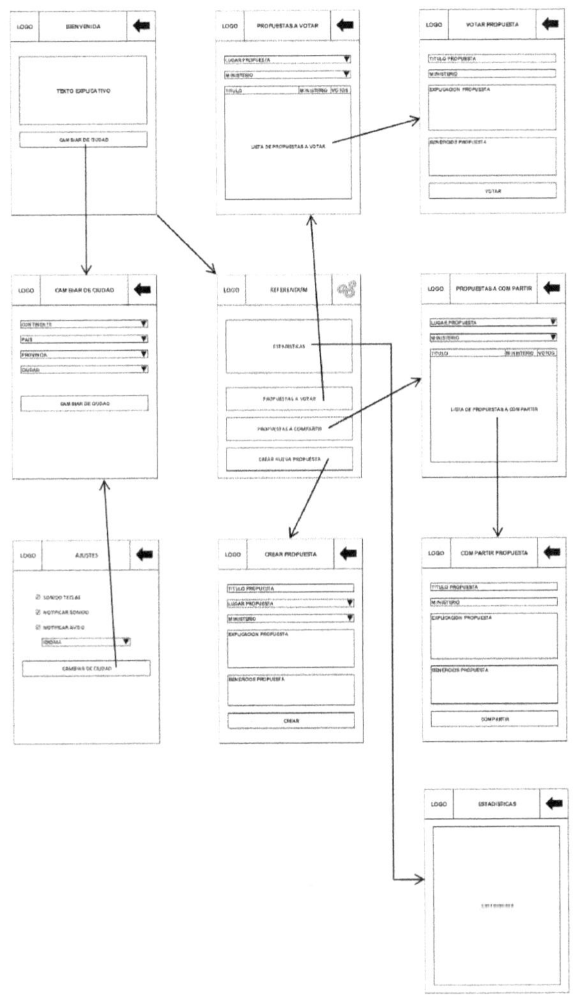

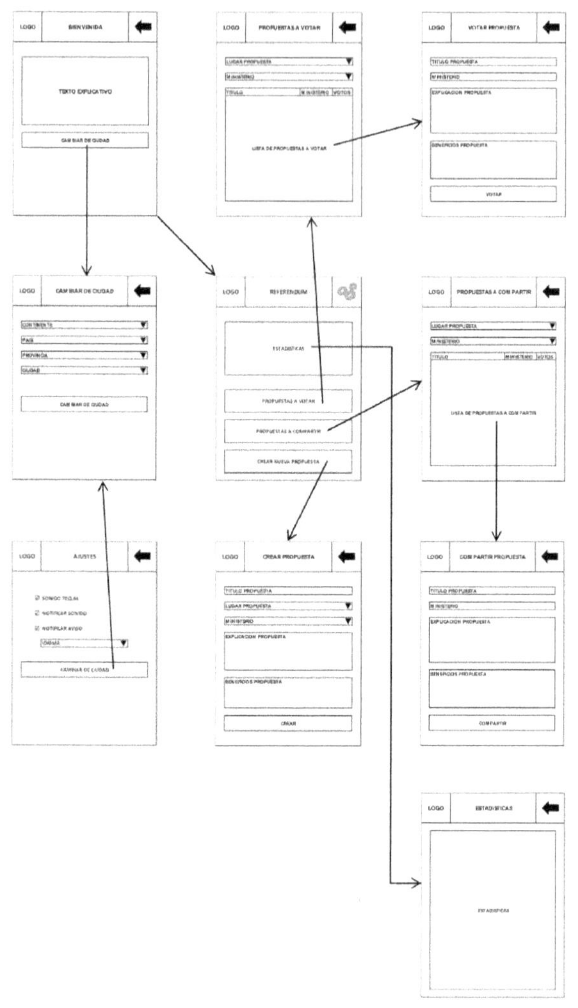

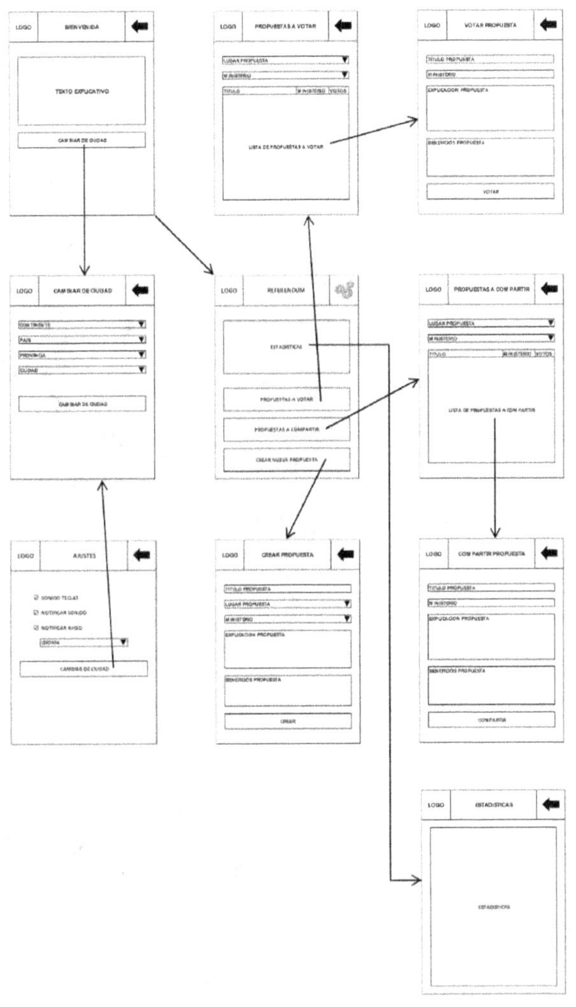